Mountains

by Susan H. Gray

Content Adviser: Terrence E. Young Jr., M.Ed., M.L.S.,
Jefferson Parish (La.) Public Schools

Reading Adviser: Dr. Linda D. Labbo,
Department of Reading Education, College of Education,
The University of Georgia

COMPASS POINT BOOKS

Minneapolis, Minnesota

Compass Point Books
3109 West 50th Street, #115
Minneapolis, MN 55410

Visit Compass Point Books on the Internet at *www.compasspointbooks.com* or e-mail your request
to *custserv@compasspointbooks.com*

Photographs ©: VCG/FPG International, cover; Index Stock Imagery, 4, 5; Internationa Stock/David E. Ward, 6; Photo
Network/Chad Ehlers, 8–9; Tom Pantages, 10; NOAA/Tom Stack and Associates, 12–13; Brian Parker/Tom Stack and
Associates, 14 top; International Stock/Warren Faidley, 14 bottom; VCG/FPG International, 15; Photo Network/Phyllis Picardi,
16; International Stock/Wayne Aldridge, 17; Visuals Unlimited/J. Creager, 18; Visuals Unlimited/Henry W. Robinson, 19;
Craig Lovell, 20; Galen Rowell/Corbis, 21; James P. Rowan, 22; J. Lotter/Tom Stack and Associates, 23; Robert McCaw, 24;
James P. Rowan, 25; Root Resources/Kenneth W. Fink, 26–27; Root Resources/Stan Osolinski, 28; Index Stock Imagery, 29;
Robert McCaw. 30; Planet Earth Pictures/FPG International, 31; Photo Network/W. Tom Lewis, 32; Craig Lovell, 33; Unicorn
Stock Photos/Tommy Dodson, 34; Gary Randall, FPG International, 35; Photo Network/Bill Terry, 36; Robert McCaw, 37;
Root Resources/Alan G. Nelson, 38; Galen Rowell/Corbis, 39; Steve Warble/Mountain Magic, 40; Root Resources, 41;
Richard Price/FPG International, 42–43.

Editors: E. Russell Primm and Emily J. Dolbear
Photo Researcher: Svetlana Zhurkina
Photo Selector: Dawn Friedman
Design: Bradfordesign, Inc.

Library of Congress Cataloging-in-Publication Data
Gray, Susan Heinrichs.
    Mountains / by Susan H. Gray.
        p. cm. — (First reports)
    Includes bibliographical references and index.
    Summary: Describes the characteristics of mountainous areas and the plants and animals that
inhabit them.
    ISBN 0-7565-0021-4 (hardcover : lib. bdg.)
        1. Mountain ecology—Juvenile literature. 2. Mountains—Juvenile literature. [1. Mountain
ecology. 2. Ecology. 3. Mountains.] I. Title. II. Series.
    QH541.5.M65 G73 2000
    577.5'3—dc21   00-008531

Table of Contents

What Is a Mountain?

▲ *The Matterhorn, in Switzerland*

When you look out of your bedroom window, what do you see? Maybe you see trees, or a grassy backyard, or other houses. Or maybe you see cars whizzing up

▲ *Glacier National Park*

▲ *The forest floor of the Great Smoky Mountains, in Tennessee*

and down the street. Try looking as far as your eyes can see. Do you see a mountain?

Mountains rise high above the surrounding land. They are the highest points on Earth. The tallest mountain in the world is Mount Everest on the borders of Tibet and Nepal, north of India. Mount Everest rises 29,028 feet (8,848 meters) above the surrounding land. Many people enjoy climbing mountains, but we can learn a lot about them from ground level too.

Earth Has Layers

The mountains we see on Earth today have not always been here. Some grew slowly over millions of years. Others rose up in a very short time.

Mountains form as Earth's **crust** shifts and moves. The crust is Earth's top layer. It surrounds Earth's inner layers the way an orange peel surrounds an orange.

Earth's crust is broken into about thirty

pieces. Scientists call these pieces **plates**. Some plates are as large as a continent. Other plates are much smaller.

▲ *Mountains pushing up through the ocean form islands.*

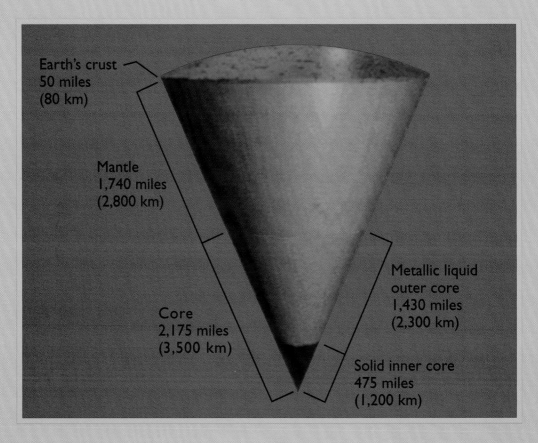

▲ *A cross-section of Earth*

Earth's crust
50 miles
(80 km)

Mantle
1,740 miles
(2,800 km)

Core
2,175 miles
(3,500 km)

Metallic liquid
outer core
1,430 miles
(2,300 km)

Solid inner core
475 miles
(1,200 km)

A thick layer called the **mantle** lies beneath Earth's crust. Earth's mantle is made up of hot, melted rock called **magma**. Magma is thick and moves slowly like toothpaste inside a tube.

Have you ever noticed that the upstairs part of a house is usually warmer than the downstairs? That happens because hot air rises. Like hot air, the hot magma deep inside Earth rises toward the surface. How does this happen?

The liquid and solid metals that make up Earth's **core** are very hot all the time. As the metals in the core give off heat, the magma closest to the core gets very hot. Then the hot magma deep inside Earth moves up toward the crust. When the hot melted rock gets close to the surface, it gives off some of its heat to the cooler crust. Then the cooler magma is forced back down toward the center of Earth as more hot magma rises to the surface. As the magma moves, it takes Earth's plates along with it.

The magma in Earth's mantle moves very slowly. Earth's plates move very slowly too.

How Do Mountains Form?

Sometimes plates move apart and tear a giant hole in Earth's crust. Magma from the mantle then moves up and fills the hole. As time passes, the magma cools

▲ *A map showing Earth's mountain ranges, on land and undersea*

and builds up in layers. These layers created the Mid-Atlantic Ridge in the middle of the Atlantic Ocean. The Mid-Atlantic Ridge is an underwater mountain chain that runs from Iceland to Antarctica.

If underwater mountains grow tall enough, they

break through the surface of the water. This is how many islands formed. The Hawaiian Islands are the tops of old volcanoes.

When magma erupts through an opening on land, scientists call it "lava." As the lava cools and hardens, it forms a mountain called a volcano. Lava may seep out over land very slowly, or it may blow out suddenly in a violent explosion. The most

Koko Head, a Hawaiian volcano

A volcano erupting

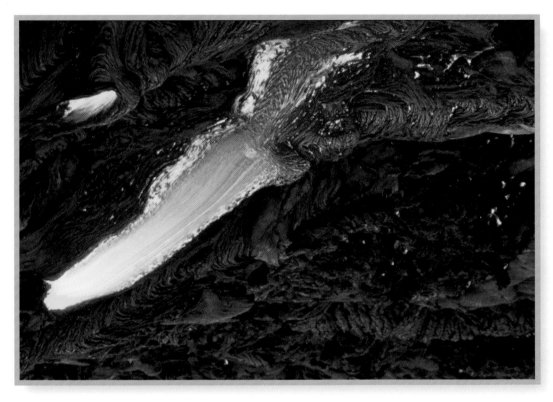

▲ Molten lava from a volcano

famous volcano in the United States is Mount Saint Helens in the state of Washington.

When two of the plates in Earth's crust collide, the edge of one may slide under the edge of the other. Then the plate on the bottom slides below the surface and becomes part of the mantle. Sometimes, one plate does not slide under the other plate.

▲ *Mount Saint Helens erupting*

Instead the two plates crash and grind. The rock that makes up the plates is pushed up and forms a mountain. This is how the Rocky Mountains formed.

▲ *A stream erodes the rock in the Canadian Rocky Mountains.*

Mountains Change over Time

Some mountains grow a little taller each year. Other mountains are shrinking. These changes are so small that we usually don't notice them.

Mount Everest is the tallest mountain in the world and each year it gets a little taller. As the Eurasian Plate moves south and the Indian-Australian Plate moves north, the land is pushed up.

▲ *Mount Everest*

▲ *The Ozarks of Arkansas*

Meanwhile, the Appalachian Mountains in the eastern United States shrink a little each year. These mountains formed millions of years ago. Heavy rains and strong winds slowly wear down, or **erode**, the mountains. The Ozarks of Arkansas are another example of mountains changed by erosion.

Sometimes mountains change a lot in hours. Years of erosion can weaken rock and cause a sudden **land-slide**. A major landslide destroys everything in its path. **Avalanches** also change the face of a mountain quickly and cause a lot of damage.

▲ *A mudslide in California deposits rock, trees, and debris on a highway.*

▲ *An avalanche*

Mountain Plants

The plants at the bottom of a mountain are very different from the plants at the top. Many plants can live at the bottom of a mountain, but few can live at the top. Usually the air temperature at the bottom of a mountain is warmer and the soil is richer.

▲ Trees in the Blue Ridge Mountains in Virginia, part of the Appalachian Mountains

▲ *A meadow at the base of Mount Mystery in Washington's Olympic National Park*

▲ *Moss growing above the tree line*

Many kinds of leafy trees grow near the bottom of a mountain. These trees lose their leaves in the winter and grow new ones in the spring. Ferns, wildflowers, moss, and grasses blanket the ground.

▲ Evergreen trees in a canyon of the Canadian Rocky Mountains

Farther up the mountain, leafy trees disappear. The land is covered with evergreens, scrubby bushes, short grasses, sedges, and heaths. Sedges are short flowering plants that keep soil from eroding. Heaths are bushy plants. Azaleas, blueberry plants, and heather are well-known heaths.

Near the tree line, it is too dry, windy, and cold for trees to grow well. These trees are knotted and stunted. Their trunks and twisted branches lie

▲ The tree line in the Sierra Nevada Mountains, California

▲ *Lichens growing on rocks*

along the ground. Clusters of trees form mats so thick that mountain climbers can walk on top of them.

An area called the alpine tundra lies above the tree line. Only a few grasses, sedges, and heaths can survive the harsh weather there. Lichens are found throughout the tundra.

Beyond the tundra, the mountains are covered in ice and snow. The air is too cold for plants to survive. Some mountains are not tall enough to have tundra or snow-capped peaks. Many smaller mountains are entirely covered in trees.

▲ *Mount McKinley in Alaska is always covered with snow.*

Mountain Animals

Like the plants, the animals at the bottom of a mountain are quite different from the animals at the top. Many kinds of animals live in burrows, caves, fields, or trees near the bottom of a mountain. Birds find plenty

▲ *A nutcracker*

▲ *An Alaskan brown bear and its cubs*

▲ *Spring peeper tree frogs live in the Great Smoky Mountains of Tennessee.*

of seeds, fruits, leaves, and flowers there. Bears feed on berries, fish from rivers and streams, and plants. Turtles, frogs, and salamanders feed on plants and insects.

A cave set into a mountainside makes a good

▲ *A cave at the base of a mountain makes a good home for many kinds of animals.*

▲ *Bats living in a cave in Indonesia*

home for salamanders, spiders, and bats. A dry rocky ledge is the perfect spot for a lizard to soak up warm rays of sunlight. Alpine meadows of heath and sedge are homes for butterflies, and other insects.

Farther up the mountain, the air is cooler. Turtles, snakes, frogs, and salamanders cannot survive there. Birds and small mammals that eat nuts, seeds, or fruit cannot find food there, so they do not live in this environment. The meat-eaters that eat birds, mice, and squirrels are rare too.

Only a few kinds of animals can survive above the tree line. They include mountain goats, bighorn sheep, and alpine ibexes. These animals have warm,

▲ *Mountain goats*

▲ *Bighorn sheep can survive above the tree line.*

thick coats. They eat the tough grasses that sprout up between the rocks. And they can leap across rough, craggy hillsides because the hooves on their feet are cushioned.

In North America, marmots and pikas live in the alpine tundra areas near the tops of tall mountains. Pikas are small mammals. They are related to rabbits.

▲ Pikas are related to rabbits.

▲ *A yellow-bellied marmot*

Pikas gather grasses in the summer and fall, and lay them out in the sun. Later, they bunch the grasses into tiny stacks and store them for winter. Marmots are large, chubby animals related to mice and beavers.

Above the alpine tundra, no animal can survive. There are no plants to eat, and very little oxygen to breathe. Only one animal ever ventures onto the ice-covered

▲ Jim Whittaker, the first American to climb Mount Everest, wearing an oxygen mask

peaks of mountains—humans. Mountain climbers survive by bringing their own food to eat and bottles of oxygen to help them breathe.

Unfortunately, some mountain climbers do not always respect the mountains. Too many people leave behind trash. This trash sometimes includes empty oxygen bottles and food wrappers. Other people must then clean up the mountains by carrying out the trash.

◀ *Volunteers clean up trash left by other climbers.*

Go Climb a Mountain!

▲ *Hikers in Switzerland*

While only a few brave mountain climbers make it to the top of the highest mountains, many people enjoy hiking up smaller mountains. Some like the fresh air and the beautiful views. Others enjoy looking at the

rocks to learn how a mountain formed. Still others study the plants and animals in mountain habitats. A mountain can be a magical place, so go find one to explore!

◄ Jasper National Park, in the Canadian Rockies

Glossary

avalanche—a mixture of ice and snow that slides down the side of a mountain. Avalanches are caused by conditions that make the snow unstable.

core—the inner layer of Earth

crust—the outer layer of Earth

erode—to break down or wear away

landslide—a mixture of rock and soil that slides down the side of a mountain. It is caused by erosion.

magma—hot, melted rock

mantle—the middle layer of Earth

plates—pieces of Earth's crust

Did You Know?

- Mount McKinley in Alaska is the tallest mountain in North America. It rises 20,320 feet (6,198 meters).

- Some mountains are made up of layers of lava. There are about 500 active volcanoes in the world today.

- Many people are concerned about the future of mountain habitats. Climbers need a lot of equipment to scale tall mountains. Hikers who climb Mount Everest pay a fee to help clean up the 50-ton pile of garbage left by climbers in the past.

At a Glance

Location: All over the world

Amount of rain or snow each year: Varies from top to bottom

Description: An area of land that rises above the surrounding area

Common animals: Varies from top to bottom, includes mountain goats, bighorn sheep, alpine ibexes, marmots, and pikas

Common plants: Varies from top to bottom, includes leafy and evergreen trees, grasses, sedges, and heaths

Want to Know More?

At the Library

Fowler, Allan. *They Could Still Be Mountains*. Danbury, Conn.: Children's Press, 1997.

Jennings, Terry J. *Mountains*. Parsippany, N.J.: Silver Burdett Press, 1998.

Parker, Jane. *Mountains*. Danbury, Conn.: Franklin Watts, 1998.

Stronach, Neil. *Mountains*. Minneapolis, Minn.: Lerner, 1996.

On the Web

Official Summits of the United States

http://www.angeleschapter.org/sps/summits/usamap.htm

For a list of all the mountains of the United States

Volcano World

http://volcano.und.nodak.edu

For maps, information, and video clips about volcanoes that are erupting right now

Through the Mail

U.S. Geological Survey

USGS National Center

12201 Sunrise Valley Drive

Reston, VA 22092

To get maps of mountains in your area

On the Road

Rocky Mountain National Park

Estes Park, CO 80517

970/586-1206

To hike, bicycle, camp, ski, snowshoe, picnic, or bird-watch

Index

About the Author

Susan H. Gray holds bachelor's and master's degrees in zoology from the University of Arkansas in Fayetteville. She has taught classes in general biology, human anatomy, and physiology. She has also worked as a freshwater biologist and scientific illustrator. In her twenty years as a writer, Susan H. Gray has covered many topics and written a variety of science books for children.